101 Ways

to

Enjoy South Haven

Written and produced by

South Haven AAUW

South Haven AAUW wishes to thank
Jan Weren for her graphic design.

To order more copies of
101 Ways to Enjoy in South Haven
please email us at
SouthHaven101Ways@yahoo.com.

Volume 1
Copyright 2010

The sun glistening on deep blue water ... the inimitable flavor of freshly milled cider ... the warmth of sand on the beach ... the distinctive call of the gulls ... the enticing aroma of a newly-baked blueberry pie. When you come to South Haven, Michigan, you don't just visit, you experience it with all your senses! Although famous for its sugar sand beaches on the Lake Michigan shoreline, the South Haven area is really a four season celebration, with plenty to enjoy year round. And that's the purpose of this little book: to introduce you to the town, its traditions and its people.

We're delighted you're here. And whether you're looking to plan a day, a week or a lifetime in South Haven, this list of 101 things is sure to make you glad you've visited, and likely make you want to come back for more!

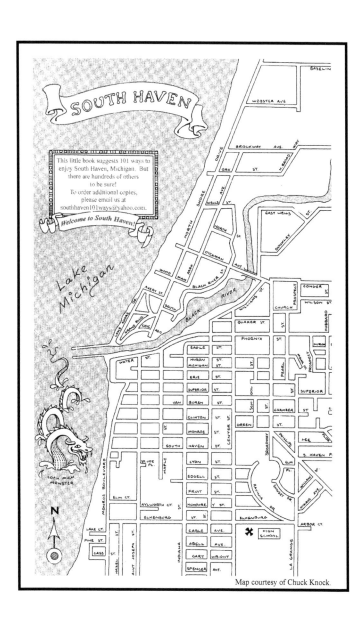

This little book suggests 101 ways to enjoy South Haven, Michigan. But there are hundreds of others to be sure!

To order additional copies, please email us at southhaven101ways@yahoo.com.

Welcome to South Haven!

SOUTH HAVEN

Lake Michigan

LOCH MICH MONSTER

N

Map courtesy of Chuck Knock.

• 1 •

Van Buren Youth Fair

You'll love this old fashioned fair, held annually the third week of July at the county fairgrounds, located in Hartford, MI. Experience a tradition that goes back 150 years promoting the best of what Van Buren county has to offer through livestock and exhibits of all kinds, be it floral, woodworking or baking.

The fairgrounds are located at 55670 CR 681 in Hartford. For more information, contact the fair office at 269-621-2038 or check out the website at www.vanburenyouthfair.com.

• 2 •

Harborfest

South Haven celebrates its harbor, and the start of the summer festival season, every June at Harborfest. Attendees enjoy live music on an outdoor stage at Riverfront Park, activities that include a Dragon Boat race, tours of the light house, a craft fair, kids' activities, and a classic boat show.

Harborfest begins Thursday evening and runs through Sunday afternoon. The South Haven Area Chamber of Commerce has details at 269-637-5171 or www.southhavenmi.com.

The Idler Riverboat and Magnolia Grill. Photo courtesy Steve Drenth.

• 3 •

Van Buren State Park

Take a hike, swim, or cross country ski along a full mile of beautiful Lake Michigan shoreline. Climb a tall dune and scan the countryside. Hike a trail through the woods. Camp in a 220 site campground. It's all available at Van Buren State Park, just five miles south of town, off Blue Star Highway and west down Ruggles Road.

Day and annual passes are available. For rates, hours and more visit www.michigandnr.com or give them a call at 269-637-2788.

• 4 •

Beach Action

South Haven's beaches are perfect for tossing a football or throwing a Frisbee. And nothing beats a game of beach volleyball! There are nets on both the North and the South beaches.

• 5 •

HarborWalk Walking Tour

What was South Haven like before the tee shirts and flip flops? Take the HarborWalk walking tour and you'll find out. A dozen historic markers along the Black River provide fascinating and informative information of the early days of this commercial and recreational harbor. Look for the framed plaques on red posts, each describing and illustrating a component of South Haven's riverfront history.

Go to
www.michiganmaritimemuseum.org/harborwalk/
for an online map of the HarborWalk
points of interest.

• 6 •

Kal-Haven Trail

Originally a railroad completed in 1870, the historic route the Kal-Haven Trail is a 33 ½ mile long, multi-use trail linking South Haven to Kalamazoo. It's a unique experience for hikers, bicyclists, nature lovers, snowmobilers, and cross-country skiers that's open year round from 8:00 am to 10:00 pm, seven days a week.

The nearest trailhead to the city is on Bailey Avenue at Wells Street, a staffed location where you can purchase passes. Phone: 269-674-8011. Refreshments and restrooms are available along the route. You'll find everything you need to know at the Van Buren County website, www.vbco.org/natfeat0014.asp.

• 7 •

Explore the Great Outdoors

Armed with field guides, animal skins, bug boxes and more, explorers young and old learn about forests, insects, ponds, plants, animals and natural features throughout Van Buren State Park. State Park guides welcome registered campers and daily visitors alike.

Nature hikes are held on Tuesdays throughout the summer. The park is located at 23960 Ruggles Road, about 5 miles south of South Haven off Blue Star Highway. More information can be found by calling 269-637-2788 or by visiting the website at www.michigandnr.com.

• 8 •

Michigan Maritime Museum

This museum, at 260 Dyckman Avenue, offers a variety of engaging opportunities, including exhibits on Michigan maritime history, a center for the teaching of boatbuilding and related maritime skills, and a regionally renowned research library. In season, the *Friends Good Will,* a historic tall ship replica, offers an unequalled opportunity to make history come alive through a variety of educational activities, including sailing her.

The museum is open year round.
Call 269-637-8078 for times or visit
www.michiganmaritimemuseum.org.
Admission is free for members, adults $5,
seniors $4 and children $3.50.

Welcome to South Haven! Photo courtesy Steve Drenth.

• 9 •

Festival of Trees

The perfect way to welcome the Christmas season! This annual event, sponsored by We Care I.N.C., begins in late November. Decorated Christmas trees are donated, after being displayed in the lower level of City Hall (539 Phoenix Street), and then sold, with proceeds going to We Care.

A Santa Parade, breakfast with the Jolly Elf, the Lego Artist Challenge, My Friend and Me Tea, the Taste of South Haven, a Senior Social Luncheon, and a PJ Popcorn Movie Night are included among the festival activities.

For all the details, visit We Care's website, www.wecare-inc.org or call them at 269 637-4342.

• 10 •

Holiday Home Tour

Set aside the first Sunday every December and join
this wonderful holiday tradition! Hospice at Home
organizes and benefits from this event, an inside
look at half a dozen South Haven area homes as
they deck their halls for the Christmas season.

The tour runs from 1:00 pm to 5:00 pm and the
ticket price includes a stop for appetizers and/or
light desserts. Hospice at Home has all the details
at 269-637-3825 or www.hospiceathomecares.org.

• 11 •

Paws on the Pier

Approximately 1,000 animal lovers – many with their canine companions – attend this event every year, usually the last Saturday in June at Riverfront Park on Water Street. Watch the canine parade, obstacle and agility courses, demonstrations, a 50/50 raffle, and much more!

Watching is free, with a fee to enter your dog in the events. All profits benefit the Al-Van Humane Society and Shelter. For more information, contact the Humane society at 269-637-5062 or visit their website at www.al-van.org.

• 12 •

The Sun Sinks Slowly into the West

And clear skies or cloudy, the sunsets in
South Haven are spectacular!

Whether you watch from the north or south beach,
either of the piers, along the river, or from a boat,
each one is a masterpiece of nature.

• 13 •

You Scream, I Scream, We All Scream for Sherman's Ice Cream

A tradition since 1957, Sherman Dairy makes ice cream the old fashioned way – loaded with natural flavors (including Michigan strawberries and blueberries and hunks of Mackinac Island fudge), one batch at a time, without any high-tech equipment. During the summer season, nearly 50 flavors are available: cones, cups, sundaes, novelties and hand-packed containers.

The dairy is located at 1601 Phoenix Road; just look for the blue cow in the roof. It's open the first Friday in March through last Sunday in October. For info call 269-637-8251 or visit www.shermanicecream.com.

• 14 •

U-Pick Fruit Farms

You could buy Lakeshore Harvest Country's bounty, or you could visit nearby farms and pick your own. The crop seasons vary by variety, but run in general from June through October. Listed are a few local farms, but a visit to www.lakeshoreharvestcountry.com will give you more complete information.

Dutch Farm Market & Bakery, 6967 109th Avenue, 269-637-8334,www.dutchfarmmarket.com; Overhiser Orchards, 6405 109th Avenue, 269-236-6312,www.overhiserorchards.com; DeGrandchamps Blueberries, 76241 14th Avenue, 269-637-3915, www.degrandchamps.com.

• 15 •

Wine Tasting

Sample the nectar of the gods right here in southwest Michigan! Enjoy these, close to South Haven, offering free tasting, plus bottles and cases for purchase.

Warner Vineyards, 515 Williams Street, www.warnerwines.com

McIntosh Orchards and Wine Cellar, 6431 107th Avenue, www.mcintoshorchards.com

Fenn Valley Vineyards, 6130 122nd Avenue, www.fennvalley.com

The South Haven Visitors' Bureau at 546 Phoenix Street has a full list of area wineries.

• 16 •

The Friends Good Will

The story of the *Friends Good Will* , a replica of an
19th century tall ship, tells of the adventures of
commerce in the early 1800's and her role
in the war of 1812. Manned by a captain and crew
dressed in period clothing,
she's a proud addition to South Haven's nautical
ties and a glorious site to see.

The ship can be toured, but a sail is the way to go,
whether by day or at sunset. She's moored at the
Maritime Museum, 260 Dyckman Avenue. Costs
vary by event and reservations can be made at
800-747-3810 or
www.michiganmaritimemuseum.org.

Friends Good Will on a sunset cruise. Photo courtesy Steve Drenth.

• 17 •

Farmers' Market

You're in the heart of Michigan's farm belt – of course you'll find a top notch Farmers' Market! Vendor tables beneath the Huron Street Pavilion display locally grown (many organically) fruits, vegetables, flowers, meats, baked goods and more. It's a festive atmosphere, with special events often accompanying the market in the adjacent park.

The market runs May through October on Wednesdays and Saturdays, from 8:00 am to 2:00 pm. There's plenty of public parking and restrooms are available. Additional information can be found at www.southhavenfarmersmarket.com or by calling 269-427-0423.

• 18 •

Gems of Yesteryear

You'll find lots of treasures in South Haven's antique stores. Murphy's Mall, located in the old Murphy Five and Dime at 321 Center Street, features more than 100 stalls.

Ambrose and Manning, 520 Phoenix Street, offers Irish goods as well as antiques. Equally intriguing is Arbor Antiques, 527 Phoenix Street.

• 19 •

Liberty Hyde Bailey Museum

The founder of modern horticulture is a native son. Liberty Hyde Bailey was born in the restored 1858 Greek Revival farmhouse, now the museum bearing his name. A National Historic site, the house and garden are open for visitors. Enjoy a self-guided stroll on the wildflower trail, maintained throughout the year, viewing over 40 native varieties of wild flowers.

The museum, at 903 S. Bailey Avenue, is open Thursday through Monday, April 1 to November 1, from 1:00 to 5:00 pm, with other times by appointment. Entry is free, but donations are gratefully accepted. For info call 269-637-3251 or visit the website, http://lhbm.south-haven.com.

• 20 •

Macdonald Drug Store

Generations of South Haven residents and visitors alike have frequented Macdonald Drug Store at 512 Phoenix Street. The store provides the downtown area's only pharmacy service and a terrific array of memorabilia to keep your South Haven memories fresh!

• 21 •

Foundry Hall

Foundry Hall is South Haven's all-ages performance venue, located at 422 Eagle Street, committed to presenting a quality mix of national, regional and local entertainment. Offering two venues, a 50 seat Red Room and a 250 seat Main Stage, you'll be delighted by musical and theatrical performances throughout the year.

Best way to get information is on their website, www.foundryhall.com, but you can also call them at 269-637-1041.

• 22 •

A Rose is a Rose...

...but a garden is so much more!

Every year the South Haven Garden Club, www.southhavengardenclub.com, sponsors the Garden Walk, a tour of five to seven private home gardens in the South Haven area. Held rain or shine, this popular event is the first Saturday after July 4th from 11:00 am to 4 pm.

Begin at the Liberty Hyde Bailey Museum, 903 South Bailey Avenue, next to the South Haven Hospital, where you can purchase tickets, enjoy refreshments and visit a garden boutique.

• 23 •

A Bicycle Built for One (or Two!)

Whether you ride your own or rent one, a bike ride around town, along the beaches, or on the Kal-Haven Trail is the perfect thing to do on a sunny day.

A weekly group rides every Thursday at 6:00 pm in the summer from Rock-n-Road at 315 Broadway (www.rocknroadcyclesouthhaven.com).

Rent bikes there, at Hotel Nichols, 201 Center Street (www.hotelnichols.com) or Outpost Sports, 124 Dyckman Street (www.outpostsports.com).

• 24 •

Sea Gulls

Their call can't help but remind us of summertime.
A number of sea gull varieties call the Great Lakes
home, each with an average life span of ten years.
Some, however, have even passed their
25th birthdays!

The males are distinguished by their red legs, and
both they and the females tend to the nest. Eggs
hatch 26 days after being laid.

Beach sentinel. Photo courtesy Judy Martens.

• 25 •

Cottage Walk

South Haven has been a summer destination for over 125 years. This is your chance to visit some of the town's original homes, cottages and resorts. Held the last Saturday in June from noon to 5:00 pm, the Cottage Walk is a fundraiser for SHOUT (South Haven Organization for United Taxpayers), a group of local volunteers who put together projects to enhance the community.

Tickets are $15 and available on the day of the event at the gazebo in Dyckman Park. The South Haven Visitor's Bureau has more information at 800-SO-HAVEN or www.southhaven.org.

• 26 •

Don Your Lederhosen!

The Downtown Association of South Haven
(D.A.S.H.) celebrates fall harvest with the
Harvest Moon Gathering
the entire month of October.
A host of traditional fall activities are featured:
Scarecrows on Parade; Apple Pie Social;
Blue Coast Artist Fall Tour; Knights of Columbus
Pancake Breakfast; SHAES Fun Fair; South Haven
Ghost Tours' Rock n' Road Boo on your Bike;
Ghouls, Doodles, Giggles & Goblins at South
Haven Art Center; SHAES's Haunted House.

Most of these hauntingly amusing activities are
free, or carry just a nominal charge.
Contact D.A.S.H. for more details at 269-639-0716.

• 27 •

Summer Concerts

There's nothing better than music under the stars. And South Haven's Riverfront Park on Water Street is the perfect venue. You can enjoy free concerts every Thursday at 7:00 pm from late May through August. Special concerts are always held during the summer festivals.

No need for reservations – just bring a blanket or a lawn chair and claim your spot on the lawn. Popcorn & beverages are available for purchase and restrooms are also available. Schedules are available at www.southhavenmi.com or www.southhaven.org or by calling 269-637-0700.

• 28 •

Scott Club Soup Luncheon

South Haven's historic Scott Club, a beautiful Queen Anne building, built by local artisans in 1893, is the location of this annual event, held the Saturday before Thanksgiving. The public is invited to enjoy a variety of delicious soups and desserts between 11:00 am and 2:00 pm. Take-out meals are available too.

The club is located at 652 Phoenix Street, with parking available across Phoenix Street in the church lot. Enter on the ground floor on the east side of the building. Call 269-639-1120 for more details.

• 29 •

Steelheaders Fish Boil

A fish boil is one of those things you have to see to believe. Enormous kettles, packed with fresh, local fish, potatoes and onions, boiling on an open fire. No wonder it attracts hundreds every Blueberry Festival.

Held on the Friday of the festival at the pavilion on Huron Street, behind the Post Office, it begins at 4:00 pm and ends when the food is gone. More information is available at www.blueberryfestival.com.

• 30 •

Ahoy, Matey!

The South Haven Yacht Club offers an array of children's sailing programs throughout the summer. In the Intro to Sailing course, students learn the basic principles of boat handling and seamanship. In the Advanced Sailing course, students work on more advanced principles of sailing. All Classes are taught by a US Sailing Certified instructor and boats are provided.

Although the Yacht Club is private, sailing classes and some social programs and events are open to the public. The club is located at 401 Williams Street, on the river. Call 269-637-2305 for more details and costs, or visit their website at www.southhavenyachtclub.com.

• 31 •

What a Peach!

The Haven peach varieties were developed right here in South Haven at Michigan State University's Experiment Station under the direction of Professor Stanley Johnston. From 1924 to 1963, Johnston combined the best features of available peach strains to create eight new, yellow-fleshed, freestone varieties. The result of his hard work are the most widely grown peaches in the world.

South Haven honored this peach of a man by naming a city park for him.

Visit Stanley Johnston Park at

220 Dyckman Avenue.

• 32 •

Hit the Waves!

Don't just look at the water, jump in! And if you're
looking for something more than just a dip,
try paddle boarding, surfing, skim boarding and
kite boarding.   Area rentals are available.

Stop in at the South Haven Visitors' Bureau at
546 Phoenix Street for rental information.

Waiting for the perfect wave. Photo courtesy Judy Martens.

• 33 •

Geocaching

geo-cash-ing – (noun): a worldwide game of hiding and seeking treasure. The basic idea is to locate hidden containers (called geochaches) using GPS technology and then share your experiences online. If there are mementos hidden, you can take one and leave one of your own. When you find a hidden cache, sign the logbook with your name, the date, and a few words about your experience.

And there are dozens of geocache locations within a few miles of South Haven! It's a great family activity. Get more information at www.geochaching.com.

• 34 •

What's a Dragon Boat and Why Are They Racing?

A dragon boat is a long boat, similar to a gondola, which seats 20 paddlers in pairs of ten, and features a dragon head on the front and its tail on the back. A drummer helps keep the paddlers in rhythm and during Harborfest in June, those drums are heard up and down the Black River, where crowds gather to watch the teams compete. The races begin on Saturday at 8:00 am and end on Sunday afternoon when winners are announced.

The South Haven Area Chamber of Commerce has Dragon Boat Race details at www.southhavenmi.com or at 269-637-5171.

• 35 •

The Blueberry Festival Arts and Crafts Fair

Artists from around the country never miss this fair and you shouldn't either!

Set in Stanley Johnston Park, at the corner of Park Street and Dyckman Avenue, this two day fair attracts craftspeople, whose mediums include paint, clay, fabric, precious metals, and more. And you won't go hungry either – with everything from fresh squeezed lemonade to fire roasted corn-on-the-cob.

Always the second weekend in August, the Arts and Crafts Fair runs Saturday from 10:00 am to 5:00 pm and Sunday from 10:00 am to 4:00 pm. More information at the Chamber of Commerce website, www.southhavenmi.com or call them at 269-637-5171.

• 36 •

Best Buy on Books

The annual AAUW Used Book Sale is a sale of gargantuan size! Thousands of books are sorted by genre, including an entire room devoted to children's books. There's no charge for browsing, but serious readers ante up $10 for early admission on Friday. Parking is free and most books are priced at $1.

The sale is always held the Friday and Saturday morning of the National Blueberry Festival, (the second full weekend in August) at the First Congregational Church, 651 Phoenix Street.

• 37 •

Kids' Corner Playground

This beautiful wooden play structure was designed and built in the '80's by the children and adults of South Haven. Kids of all ages love the maze, boat, slides, rope bridge, tire bridge, and more.
Also on the premises are a ball diamond, picnic tables, and restrooms.

The playground is on Monroe Boulevard between Monroe Street and South Haven Street. Open year round from dawn till 10 pm, with plenty of free street parking.

• 38 •

Mother Nature at Her Finest

The Sarett Nature Center is a 1,000+ acre wildlife sanctuary with over 5 miles of maintained walking and skiing trails. Wonderful weekend programs are offered, with naturalist led hikes and programs for both adults and children.

Open Tuesday through Friday, the center charges $3 for adults, but children under 12 are free, as are members. Located at 2300 Benton Center Road, the center is south of South Haven, exit 1 off I-196. Head west to the first street, turn north, and travel approximately one mile. For more information, visit them at www.sarett.com, or call 269-927-4832.

• 39 •

Story Time

The South Haven Memorial Library offers preschool story hour, complete with crafts, dance, games and rhymes, every Tuesday at 11:00 am. And during the summer, early elementary school students are invited to their own story hour, also on Tuesdays at 11:00 am.

The story hours are free of charge, and parents are asked to attend with their preschool children. For information and the week's theme, give the library a call at 269-637-2403 or visit them on line at www.shmlibrary.org. The library is located at 314 Broadway Street, next to the post office.

• 40 •

Historical Association of South Haven

Located in the century-old Hartman School House, the Historical Association of South Haven (HASH) sponsors exhibits and events highlighting the community's history, plus offering free programs to the public. HASH also sponsors the Bark Peelers, a Vintage Baseball Team that maintains a schedule of free games during the summer.

HASH is located at 355 Hubbard Street, one block south of Phoenix Street and is open from June 1 to October 31 on Sundays, 2:00 to 4:00 pm. It's also open for special displays and programs throughout the year. Entry is free, but donations are gratefully accepted. Visit them at www.historyofsouthhaven.org.

• 41 •

Light Up the Lake

There's no better way to celebrate our nation's independence than watching spectacular fireworks along the shores of Lake Michigan! Shot off from the south pier, there are vantage points on both the north and south sides of the river to watch this pyrotechnics display. Better still, take a boat into the lake and view the thrilling show overhead. Add another dimension to your celebration by tuning into local radio station 103.7 COSY-FM for choreographed music.

The date varies, so verify it on the South Haven Visitors' Bureau website (www.southhaven.org). The show starts at dusk, but find your viewing spot early.

The lake lights up on the 4th of July. Photo courtesy Kelly Weber.

• 42 •

Cranberries in Michigan?

You bet! DeGrandchamp's Farm, just three miles south of town at Blue Star Highway and 14th Avenue, has 30 acres of cranberries. Every fall, between September and October, the beds are flooded and the fruit is "beaten" off the vine using a specialized harvester. The floating fruit is then corralled and loaded onto trucks to become juice and sauce.

Best of all, you can take a wagon ride through these cranberry bogs. Call the farm – 269-637-3915 – or visit their website – www.degrandchamps.com – to confirm dates, times and prices.

• 43 •

Build Yourself a Castle

A sand castle that is! Michigan's beautiful, white sugar sand beaches are perfect for castles or any other sculpture your imagination can conjure up. You'll find all the resources you need right at the water's edge.

And don't miss the Sand Sculpture Contest, Sunday of the Blueberry Festival, the second weekend in August. The contest is held on the North Beach and is open to groups or individuals. The Blueberry Festival website has all the details at www.blueberryfestival.com.

• 44 •

Battle the Pirates

South Haven's tall ship, the *Friends Good Will*, isn't just for fun. She patrols the lakefront, protecting the good citizens of South Haven from marauding pirates! Children large and small are given hats and swords, and then help haul the sails. And once the pirates are defeated and the treasure chest is brought on board, everyone shares in the bounty.

The ship sails from the dock at the Maritime Museum, 260 Dyckman Avenue. For more information, call 269-637-8078 or visit their website at www.michiganmaritimemuseum.com.

• 45 •

Blue Coast Artists Studio Tour

For over twenty years the Blue Coast Artists have been delighting and educating the public with their annual Fall Tour of Studios the first weekend in October. The tour includes several working artists' studios located between South Haven and Saugatuck.

Each site features demonstrations, original artwork, refreshments and more. Hands-on art making projects, unique art abodes and fall color makes this creative experience fun for the whole family.

A tour map is available on the website at www.bluecoastartists.com.

• 46 •

Miniature Golf

If full size golf is over your head, try out something more your size at Lakeside Entertainment's Miniature Golf Course. Its 18 holes are designed to be challenging without the obstacles of a putt-putt course, but landscaped with ponds, fountain, stream and waterfall. Cost is just $5.00 for adults, $4.00 for juniors and seniors.

The course, at the corner of M-40 and Blue Star Highway, opens at noon. Call for more information, 269-637-6500, or visit www.lakesidebowl.com.

• 47 •

Chase the Winter Blues Away!

And that's exactly what happens at the annual Ice Breaker Festival, the first weekend of February (Friday through Sunday). The annual activities include professional ice carvings, free chili cook-off samples throughout downtown, free ice skating lessons, free arts and crafts for kids at library and art center, free horse wagon rides, free skating team performance, a Mardi Gras dinner, a Texas Hold 'Em tournament, a pancake breakfast, and fabulous sales at many downtown stores.

The South Haven Area Chamber of Commerce will give you all the details at 269-637-5171 or on their website at www.southhavenmi.com.

• 48 •

U Pick 'Em

You're in the self-proclaimed National Blueberry Capital, you gotta spend some time picking your own! And DeGrandchamp's Farm is South Haven's largest and closest blueberry U-Pick, with 130 acres of those little blue gems just three miles south of town at Blue Star Highway and 14th Avenue.

Visit their Farm Market, tour the packing plant, peruse the nursery division and go home happy! U-Pick dates are July through August; the market is open July through November. For exact times, call 269-637-3915 or check out their site, www.degrandchamps.com.

Bounty of the National Blueberry Capital. Photo courtesy Judy Martens.

• 49 •

Volksmarch

A volksmarch is a walk – it's not competitive and not a race. Do it with a club, your family ... or all by yourself, and there are thousands of volkssport clubs around the world. The 10 km South Haven trail is on paved roads and sidewalks, by quaint shops, through historic neighborhoods and along the shores of Lake Michigan.

The volksmarch can be taken April through November, starting at Café Julia, 561 Huron Street. Ask the staff for the volksmarch file box. Please note that the route is not suitable for strollers or wheelchairs. For more information, visit the volksmarch website at www.ava.org/clubs/pathwalkers.

• 50 •

Sailing, sailing ....

Enjoy the magnificence of Lake Michigan aboard a beautiful sailboat. Local captains are happy to charter a cruise for your family or group and a view of Lake Michigan's shoreline from her clear waters is a sight to remember. You can even arrange for a picnic on board!

See the Boating and Cruises link at www.southhaven.org to choose the cruise that is best for you.

• 51 •

South Haven High School Stars

Remember how much fun your high school drama class was? And remember how wonderful it was to have a full audience to play to? Here's your chance to give back by attending one of the school performances in the fall
(the weekend before Thanksgiving)
or spring (the 1st or 2nd weekend in March).

All performances are held at Listiak Auditorium at the high school, 600 Elkenburg Street. Call for information, 269-637-0502, or visit the school's website at www.shps.org.

• 52 •

The Allegan Antique Market

Held the last Sunday of each month, April through
September, this antique market features 400 dealers
spread across the Allegan County Fairgrounds
(just off of M-89 and M-40 in the city of Allegan).

The market is open rain or shine,
from 8 am to 4 pm. Admission is $4.00,
but parking is free. Visit their website at
www.alleganantiques.com or call 616-735-3333
for more information.

• 53 •

The Barkpeelers

Hurray for the Barkpeelers, South Haven's own vintage baseball team. The 1880's costumed team banters with the audience, explains the old baseball rules, and provides great family entertainment.

Home games are played at the ball field west of Kids' Corner, on Monroe Blvd. between Monroe Street and South Haven Street. Dates can be found at the Historical Association of South Haven website, www.historyofsouthhaven.org/events.php.

• 54 •

Great Lakes History

The Marialyce Canonie Great Lakes Research Library is the only facility in the state to collect and share information on the scope of Michigan's maritime history. This collection consists of almost 4,000 books, sound recordings, maps, DVDs, charts and more.

The library is located within sight of the lighthouse, at 91 Michigan Avenue. This building served as a residence for South Haven lighthouse keepers and their families from 1872 until 1939. Open to the public year round on Thursdays from 10:00 am to 5:00 pm, or by appointment by calling 269-637-9156 or visiting www. michiganmaritimemuseum.org.

South Haven lighthouse. Photo courtesy Steve Drenth.

• 55 •

A-Mazing Corn

Ever hear of a corn maze? Even if you have,
you've never seen one like this! Crane Orchards,
located in Fennville about 20 miles north of
South Haven, boasts one of the state's best. It's a
fall tradition not to be missed. Their website,
www.craneorchards.com, will give you dates, times
and directions, along with a-mazing pictures of
mazes past.

• 56 •

GingerMan Race Track

Looking for car racing excitement? GingerMan offers a weekend escape that's a chance to feel life with your senses as well as the seat of your pants! Drive your car at open track or just watch the fun. Check out the racing event schedule at www.gingermanraceway.com.

GingerMan is open every season but winter and is located approximately 6 miles east of town at 61414 Phoenix Road.

• 57 •

On Your Mark ... get set...

... go! The Blueberry Festival 5k takes runners
through beautiful downtown South Haven and
along the picturesque shores of Lake Michigan.
Medals go to the top three competitors in
each age group.

The race is always the Saturday of
Blueberry Festival (second weekend every August),
begins at the Municipal Marina, 345 Water Street
and starts at 8:00 am. Registration is $20. Call
800-SO-HAVEN (764-2836), or visit
www.blueberryfestival.com, for details.

• 58 •

Petoskey Stones

Michigan's official state stone, the Petoskey stone
is actually fossilized coral and found only on the
shores of Lake Michigan and Lake Huron.

The word *petoskey* comes from the name of an
Ottawa Indian chief, Petosegay, meaning
"rays of dawn." Polished Petoskey stones make
beautiful jewelry, found in many area
shops and galleries.

• 59 •

Commune with Mother Nature

The South Haven area boasts many parks that offer visitors myriad year-round activities. Spring brings nature walks and bird watching, summer provides swimming, boating, canoeing, kayaking, hiking, bird-watching, metal detecting, and biking.

In the Fall, there's camping and hunting (in designated areas) and winter offers plenty of snow for cross-country skiing and snowmobiling fun.

Find the best park for your needs at www.southhaven.com/south-haven-mi-parks.

Area woods shine in all seasons. Photo courtesy Kelly Weber.

• 60 •

National Blueberry Festival

Michigan produces more than 220,000 tons of blueberries every year, the lion's share of which are grown in the South Haven area. We celebrate this little blue gem with the annual, four-day National Blueberry Festival. The celebration includes activities for all ages: a parade, concerts, a 5K run, a sand sculpture contest at the beach, an air-show at the municipal airport, fundraiser dinners, sidewalk sales, a pie eating contest, an arts and crafts fair, an antique flea-market, and more.

The festival is held the second weekend in August. Find more information at www.blueberryfestival.com.

• 61 •

Michigan Flywheelers Museum

Run by a group of volunteers dedicated to the restoration and preservation of antique gas and steam engines and tractors, this museum is home to many operating displays and some great events. Stop by the Swap Meet the second weekend in June or Michigan's largest annual Antique Engine and Tractor Show, held each September.

The museum is open Memorial Day to Labor Day, Wednesdays and weekends from 10:00 am to 3:00 pm and is located at 06285 68th Street, ½ mile south of Phoenix Road. You can reach them at 269-639-2010 or online, www.michiganflywheelers.org.

• 62 •

South Haven Center for the Arts

Located at 600 Phoenix Avenue, in a building built in 1906 with a gift from Andrew Carnegie, this community art center offers exhibits of regional and local art. In addition, there are classes for adults and children, with special events throughout the year
(don't miss the Mistletoe Market in December!).

The center is open year round, Mondays noon to 5:00 pm, Tuesdays through Fridays 10:00 am to 5:00 pm, Saturdays 1:00 to 4:00 pm, and May 1 to October 31, Sundays 1:00 to 4:00 pm. Admission is free, but donations are gratefully accepted. Call for information, 269-637-1041, or visit http://southhavenarts.org.

• 63 •

Old McDonald Had a Farm...

.. and now you can tour it and enjoy some of the area's finest fruits and vegetables! The Lakeshore Harvest Country organizes activities throughout the growing season, from June through October. Visit the farms, pick your own fresh produce or purchase jams, honey, eggs and more. And don't miss the Family Farm Fest, the fourth Saturday in July, and the Road Rally, the second Saturday in October.

Farms are located north of South Haven and south of Saugatuck along the Lake Michigan shoreline. To get the full story, visit the group's website, www.lakeshoreharvestcountry.com, or call 269-270-1473.

• 64 •

Meteor Showers

Star gazing on the shores of Lake Michigan - what could be better? Watching the Perseid Meteor Showers in August, of course!   And in a small town, the ambient light is minimal, providing optimal viewing.

The showers usually peak on August 12 but a visit to the NASA website will give the most complete information at www.nasa.gov.

• 65 •

Golden Brown Bakery

Looking for the best chocolate donut this side of heaven? Look no further than South Haven's hometown bakery, making smiles since 1938. Artisan breads, baked goods of all kinds, wedding cakes and birthday cakes(requested by local kids for generations). A cafeteria with breakfast and lunch menus and great coffee make this a popular stop for locals and visitors alike.

The bakery, located in downtown South Haven at 421 Phoenix Street, is open all year, Monday through Saturday 6:00 am to 5:00 pm. Catch a preview of their treats at www.goldenbrownbakery.com.

• 66 •

Perca Flavescens

Otherwise known as yellow perch, they're South Haven's official fish and the most popular main course at many local restaurants.

Mild in flavor and delicious fried or sautéed.

Try catching your own by joining the locals on the pier. Fishing licenses, equipment and tackle are available at:

All Seasons Marine, 234 Black River Street

Dunhams, 1220 Phoenix Street

Pyles' Porthole, 141 Dunkley Avenue

Or charter your own boat through

South Haven Fishing Charters,

269-208-3545.

Fish away the summer days. Photo courtesy Steve Drenth.

• 67 •

Love will find a way...

... via a tennis game, that is!

Baseline Middle School is the place, at 7357
Baseline Road. Go north on Blue Star Highway to
Baseline Road, west on Baseline to the school.
The courts are on the north end of the school.

Play anytime from dawn to dusk, mid-June to
mid-August, when school is not in session.

• 68 •

Hurray for Hollywood

Whether it's a rainy day or romantic evening, catching first run movies at South Haven's iconic Michigan Theater (210 Center Street) is a great way to spend a couple of hours. But what's even better is the price.

All shows before 6 pm are $4; shows after 6 pm are $5.50. The Monday special is two tickets for $8.00, and all ticket prices include pop and popcorn (with purchase of a bucket).

Check titles and show times at 269-637-1662.

• 69 •

A Floating Outhouse?

See that and more at the annual Dinghy Parade,
featuring decorated dinghies and inflatables. If
you're without watercraft, then find a spot
along the river to observe.

From the serious to the hilarious – you'll not want
to miss this annual event, held at 6:00 pm the
Saturday after the 4th of July. Entrants must
register online by the previous day at noon or in
person on parade day by 5:30 p.m. at the South
Haven Yacht Club dock. There's no fee,
but registration is a must.

Get all the details at www.shdinghyparade.com.

• 70 •

Michigan Blueberry Chutney

1 C chopped onion

½ C dried cranberries or cherries

2 T butter

½ C raisins

1 ½ C washed blueberries

¼ C brown sugar

½ C apple cider vinegar

1 t salt

1 t Chinese Five Spices or cinnamon

Lightly cook onions in butter in a medium sauce pan.
Add all remaining ingredients and bring to an easy boil.
Reduce heat and simmer 15 to 20 minutes, stirring often
to a thick consistency. Can be stored in the fridge for up
to a week or freezer for several months. Fabulous on
top of warmed Brie and served with crostini
or firm crackers.

• 71 •

The Scott Club

Named for the 19th century author Sir Walter Scott, this women's reading circle was founded in 1883. The club merged with the Literary and Antiquarian Societies, and in 1892, the cornerstone of the sandstone Queen Anne structure at 652 Phoenix Street was laid.

The building was designed by John Cornelius Randall, built by local artisans and completed in 1893. Its two Austrian stained glass windows portray Sir Walter Scott and Henry Wadsworth Longfellow. The building has been in continuous use by the Scott Club as a cultural center providing fellowship for women and became a Michigan Historical Site in 1982.

• 72 •

Plying the Waters of the Black River

The Heritage Water Trail is a 21 mile canoe and
kayak trek down the south branch of the
Black River between Bangor and South Haven.
You can enjoy the river trail from dawn to dusk,
and there are even periodic paddle events.

There's no cost if you have your own boat, and the
South Haven Chamber of Commerce or the South
Haven Visitors Bureau can provide you with canoe
and kayak rental information. Launch sites and
information is available at
www.vbco.org/watertrail.asp.

The mouth of the Black River. Photo courtesy Kelly Weber.

• 73 •

Invite a Duck to Lunch

The Black River is home to a very large (and very
friendly) duck population. And they love the
attention and goodies from their human neighbors.
Spend an afternoon making some new friends by
sharing popcorn or bread crumbs with them.

The best spot is at Riverfront Park on Water Street.
The ducks won't even mind if you snap
a photo or two!

• 74 •

The South Haven Lighthouse

Of the more than 250 lighthouses in Michigan, South Haven's is one of the most beautiful and accessible. Join the joggers and strollers on the pier, and be sure to bring your camera!

You can tour inside the lighthouse during June's Harborfest. Check out www.southhavenharborfest.com.

• 75 •

Chili Cook Off

Fancy yourself a chili aficionado? Then the annual
Chili Cook Off is for you, taking place from noon
to 3:00 pm during Ice Breaker Festival
(the first weekend of February). Downtown
restaurants and businesses vie for top honors with
the public voting based on free samples!

There's also an amateur version held at Foundry
Hall, with awards presented at 5:30 pm on
Saturday. Entry fee is $25 and samples are
25 cents each.

More information is available from the South
Haven Area Chamber of Commerce,
269-637-5171, and We Care, INC, 269-637-4342.

• 76 •

I Love a Parade

And so do the good people of South Haven! Join
the crowds to watch bands, military units, scouts,
local personalities, acrobats, antique vehicles,
clowns, fire engines, beauty queens, floats, and
representatives from area businesses, churches,
athletic teams, and civic organizations.

The city's parades include Memorial Day,
Independence Day, Blueberry Festival,
and the Santa Parade.

Contact the South Haven Visitors Bureau
(800-SO-HAVEN or www. southhaven.org)
to learn about the next parade. Maybe you can
form your own entry and march along!

• 77 •

Ice Skating

Think Currier and Ives. Think romantic movies.
Then think ice skating under the Huron Street
pavilion in downtown South Haven! It's a favorite
winter activity from Thanksgiving to March with
Mother Nature's cooperation.

Skate rentals, refreshments and restrooms are
available. One day passes and skate rentals are
$3.50 each and a season pass is $60. For hours and
information, call 269-639-1113, or visit the website
at www.shicerink.com.

• 78 •

Fore!

If you're looking to get your golf game on, we've got fore (4) excellent choices! Each one provides challenges for all levels and each affords beautiful views of Mother Nature's handiwork!

HawksHead Links: Open 7 days a week, April through October, 269-639-2121, www.hawksheadlinks.com.

Beeches Golf Club: Open April through October, 269-637-2600, www.beechesgolfclub.com.

Glen Shores Golf Course: Open April through October, 269-227-3226, www.glennshores.com.

South Haven Golf Club: Open April through October, 269-637-3896.

• 79 •

Attention Budding Artists!

The South Haven Art Center invites you to show off your imagination and expression at a drop-in art class. These one hour creative sessions are taught by artists and certified art teachers and are designed for children (or children at heart) four and older.

There are new projects every day, but class size is limited, so it's best to plan ahead. Art classes are held late June through early August, Tuesday through Friday.

The South Haven Art Center is located at 600 Phoenix Street.
For times and fees, call at 269 637-1041 or visit www.southhavenarts.org.

• 80 •

The South Haven Memorial Library

You'll love this friendly, small-town library! There's a summer reading program for children, an outstanding children's library, plus a separate area for teens. Library programs for all ages are announced on the library bulletin board or the website, www.shmlibrary.org.

If you'll be in town for a while, consider the one-month card that permits access to the entire collection of books, magazines, and videos. Computers with internet access are available and the entire building has Wi-Fi. Hours vary by day and season; for information, call 269-637-2403. The library is located at 314 Broadway Street, next to the post office.

• 81 •

A Drive through History

Every summer, in celebration of the town's resort history, the Historical Association of South Haven (HASH) sponsors a driving tour. A published guide available at Lakeshore Framing and Artwork,
263 Broadway Street,
features a centerfold map of the South Haven area marking the locations of 42 former Jewish resorts, with pictures and a short history of each.

The tour is self-directed, with numbered signs coinciding with the places on the map posted at each location. More information is available at the HASH website, www.historyofsouthhaven.org.

• 82 •

Moonlight Becomes You

There's nothing more magical than strolling along
the Lake Michigan shoreline under a full moon.
Take your loved one's hand a make a memory
that will last a lifetime!

Strolling the south pier. Photo courtesy Judy Martens.

• 83 •

Bowl On

What to do on a rainy day? Have a bowling party! Lakeside Entertainment off M-40 at the corner of Blue Star Highway offers 16 lanes, plus arcade games and good eats. And when the sun comes out again, there's also a miniature golf course.

Lakeside opens at noon and is open all year long. For more information, call 269.637.6500 or go to www.lakesidebowl.com.

• 84 •

Pancake Breakfasts

It's a South Haven tradition. And the Kiwanis and Rotary clubs know how to throw excellent pancake breakfasts – mouth watering cakes, crisp bacon, savory sausage and gallons of great coffee!

The breakfasts are in conjunction with area festivals. Times and locations are always well advertised.

Most are held in town with exception of the Sunday Blueberry Festival Breakfast, held at the South Haven Regional Airport, 3.5 mi. south on M140, 0.8 mi. east on CR380 at 73020 County Road 389. It coincides with a Fly-In that attracts pilots and aircraft enthusiasts from a wide region.

• 85 •

Sail into the Sunset

A Lake Michigan sunset is a thing to behold. And
viewing it from the decks of the tall ship
Friends Good Will will make a memory
you'll never forget!

The ship sails from the Michigan Maritime
Museum dock for sunset cruises throughout the
summer months. For times and information, call
them at 269-637-8078, or visit their website,
www.michiganmaritimemuseum.com.

• 86 •

One Person's Junque is Another's Treasure

And Sunset Junque is one of the most unique treasure vendors you'll stumble upon. Located 5 miles north of South Haven at 856 Blue Star Highway, this is a collector's dream, with indoor and outdoor displays.

Sunset is open daily Memorial Day to Labor Day, and weekends in the off season. Take a virtual tour at www.sunsetjunque.com or call 269-637-5777 for more information.

• 87 •

Our Town Players

Whether you watch or participate, you're sure to
enjoy the productions of
the South Haven Area Community Theatre. Their
work includes a Winter Children's Production,
the Short and Sweets presented in April and May,
and a Summer Production.

Overcome your stage fright – contact Our Town
Players at 269-639-8228 or
www.ourtownplayers.org.

• 88 •

A Horse, A Horse, My Kingdom for a Horse!

As one of Southwestern Michigan's largest horse farms, Willow Tree Equestrian Center has everything a horse enthusiast could want on its sprawling 100 plus acres.   The indoor arena is used year-round for lessons, shows and events, and there are plenty of trails for pleasure riding.

Willow Tree is located off M-43 about 6 miles east of town. Visit their website, www.i2k.com/~willow, or call them at 269-427-5141 for more information.

Winter frolics. Photo courtesy Kelly Weber.

• 89 •

Smooth Sledding in South Haven!

Bring your toboggans, sleds, saucers, whatever for
an old-fashioned day on snowy hills. You'll want
to bring a thermos of hot chocolate along –
these hills are the real deal!

Best sledding spots are at the corner of Michigan
Avenue and St. Joseph Street (next to the Michigan
Maritime Museum Library) or at Baer Park,
the corner of Center Street and Michigan Avenue.
There are no restrooms available,
but this winter fun is free for all!

• 90 •

Everybody in the Pool!

Mid-June through mid-August, South Haven's
Community Pool offers swimming lessons for all
abilities in four summer sessions of two weeks
each, as well as Adult Lap Swimming and Water
Exercise. Then, October through February, the
South Haven Rams Aquatic Club sponsors
competitive swim meets for kids.

Lessons are $45 per session, adult exercise is $3.00
per hour. The pool is located in the southwest
corner of the South Haven High School,
at 600 Elkenburg Street. For additional information
call the pool phone at 269-637-0581,
or visit www.shps.org.

• 91 •

Explore the Shipwrecks

On November 19, 1891, the Rockaway, a scow
schooner, ran into an autumn storm. The captain
and crew, six in all, were rescued just before the
ship sank. She now lies 2 ½ miles northwest of
South Haven, rediscovered in 1983.
The Michigan Maritime Museum sponsored six
seasons of archaeological fieldwork in cooperation
with the Michigan Bureau of History and
the Department of Natural Resources.
The remains of the wreck make for an interesting
dive, just one of several in the area. Visit
www.michiganshipwrecks.org for additional
local dive sites.

• 92 •

One Book, One Community

Every winter, the city of South Haven chooses a
book upon which the entire community can focus.
The project involves lectures, demonstrations,
movies, and discussion groups that meet to share
ideas and reactions to the chosen book.

Coordinated by the South Haven Memorial Library
at 314 Broadway Street, the activities are free of
charge and take place at various locations around
town. More information is available on the
library's website, www.shmlibrary.org.

• 93 •

Black River Books

South Haven's premiere used book store,
Black River offers everything from first editions to
rare and collectibles to paper backs. Enjoy a cup of
coffee, tea or cocoa, sink into a comfortable chair,
and enjoy your library's new additions. While the
store's proprietors are delightfully helpful, the store
mascots, Labradoodles Booker and Dewey,
make the visit a treat.

Black River is open year-round at
330 Kalamazoo Street. For hours, give them a call
at 269-637-7374 or visit their website at
www.blackriverbooks.net.

• 94 •

Yeah Team!

Nothing says autumn like a high school football game, and spring is always heralded by baseball cheers. Join the hometown crowd as they gather to support local teams in every season.

Football, track and soccer occur at

Ratcliff Field, 355 Hubbard Street.

All other events are at

South Haven High School, 600 Elkenburg.

Schedules for every sport are available at www.highschoolsports.net. Tickets are available at each venue; prices vary by event.

• 95 •

Summer Art in the Park

This juried art fair takes place under the trees in historic Stanley Johnston Park (the corner of Park Street and Dyckman Avenue), named for South Haven's native son and developer of the Haven peach varieties. The fair annually draws over 100 exhibitors from across the country, with artists working in watercolors, oils, photography, textiles, jewelry, metalwork, pottery, sculpture and mixed media.

Summer Art in the Park is the first Sunday in July from 10:00 am to 5:00 pm. Exhibitor and viewer information is available from the South Haven Center for the Arts at 269-637-1041, and www.southhavenarts.org.

• 96 •

Classic Boat Show and Small Craft Festival

Row, paddle, sail and motor – all are featured afloat and on shore. Demonstrations and speakers entertain and inform throughout the day, and all kids are invited to join in the toy boat building event.

This annual event, held at the Maritime Museum at 260 Dyckman Avenue, coincides with a Traditional Small Craft Association (TSCA) National Council meeting. Contact the museum for more information: www.MichiganMaritimeMuseum.org or 269-637-8078.

• 97 •

Got Snow?

We do – every winter! So why not jump on a snowmobile and enjoy it. The 14-mile long Van Buren Trail and the Kal-Haven Trail start in South Haven and both are open in the winter for snowmobiling, passing through small towns, over bridges, and through some of Michigan's most beautiful countryside.

You won't need a Kal-Haven Trail pass but you do need a DNR Snowmobile Trail Permit. For information on both trails, go to www.vbco.org or www.michigandnr.com/parksandtrails.

North pier lighthouse in winter. Photo courtesy Kelly Weber.

• 98 •

Guilt Free Blueberry Pie

9" Pie Crust

½ tsp. Cinnamon

4 cups Blueberries

1/4 cup Flour

½ cup Sugar

½ tsp. Lemon Juice

½ cup Splenda (granulated)

1 tbsp. Butter

Line pie plate with crust. Trim excess crust and save to decorate top. Combine sugar, Splenda,cinnamon and flour. Fold in blueberries and lemon juice. Spread in pie crust. Dot top with small pieces of butter and decorate with crust trimmings. Bake one hour at 350 degrees, until crust is golden brown and filling is bubbly. Top with whipped cream or ice cream (but no guilt!).

• 99 •

Go Off the Grid

There are many things to enjoy in the South Haven
area. But sometimes you just have to go off the
grid for the day:
no TV, no telephone, no car, no computer.
Gather family and friends and
enjoy the great outdoors!

• 100 •

Apple of My Eye

Ask anyone in this area about fruit pies and they'll undoubtedly put Crane's Pie Pantry at the top of the list. Located 20 miles north of South Haven in Fennville, Crane's has been serving up pies along with lunches and dinners, since 1968.

Well worth the drive, Crane's is open year round. For hours and directions, call them at 269-561-2297 or visit their website, www.cranespiepantry.com.

• 101 •

Blueberry pie, me oh my!

Don't miss the pie eating contest, Saturdays during
the annual National Blueberry Festival
(the second weekend of August). Children compete
to see who can eat the most blueberry pie, without
using their hands. The contest is held at Riverfront
Park, along the south side of the river
on Water Street. Very messy, but lots of fun!

For more information, go to
www.blueberryfestival.com or contact
nationalbluerryfestival@gmail.com.